How To Share
The New Birth and
The Gift of the Holy Spirit

by
Frank L. Stewart

HARRISON HOUSE
Tulsa, Oklahoma

Unless otherwise indicated,
all Scripture quotations are taken from
the *King James Version* of the Bible.

7th Printing
Over 42,000 in Print

How To Share The New Birth and The Gift of the Holy Spirit
ISBN 0-89274-295-X
Copyright © 1983 by Frank L. Stewart
P. O. Box 5959D
Los Angeles, California 90059

Published by Harrison House, Inc.
P. O. Box 35035
Tulsa, Oklahoma 74153

Printed in the United States of America.
All rights reserved under International Copyright Law.
Contents and/or cover may not be reproduced in whole or
in part in any form without the express written consent
of the Publisher.

Contents

Foreword

How To Minister Salvation

Explain the need	1
Present the solution	4
Explain salvation is by grace	5
Lead candidate to receive	7
How to pray for salvation	9
How to minister assurance of salvation	10
How to pray for assurance of salvation	12

How To Minister the Gift of the Holy Spirit

Two qualifications	13
Reason for receiving	17
What candidate should expect to do	18
Lead candidate to receive by faith	19
How to pray to receive	20
Lead candidate to release utterance	20
Instruct candidate to pray in tongues daily	25

Foreword

For over twelve years I have enjoyed the inspiring friendship and fellowship of Frank Stewart. We functioned together as assistant pastors at Crenshaw Christian Center in Inglewood, California.

Able as an executive and gifted as a minister, Frank is also preeminent as a teacher. From the time he first came on staff at Crenshaw, he has been an incomparable, meticulous, Bible-believing, walking-by-faith teacher and preacher of God's Word. His knowledge and understanding of the Scriptures, as well as his appreciation of the laws of pedagogy, make him a giant in Christian leadership training. Best of all, Frank has the gift of leading others into a joyous life in Christ.

You will find that this book has the same quality. It is practical, inspirational, and filled with instruction—a great help in the Christian walk. Read it prayerfully and repeatedly. Use it not as a crutch but as the ripened instruction of a talented teacher that will help you lead others to discover the fuller knowledge and experience which is already yours.

—Dr. Edward L. Haygood, Pastor
Christian Agape Circle
Los Angeles, California

How To Minister Salvation

There are five basic Scripture references useful in ministering the plan of salvation. These should be used in this order:

1. Romans 5:12
2. John 3:16
3. Ephesians 2:8,9
4. John 1:12
5. Romans 10:9

As these verses are committed to memory in the order given, the Holy Spirit will bring to remembrance the information provided as to what each refers and how they are to be applied most effectively.

Explain the need for salvation.

The candidate should understand the need for salvation. Romans 5:12 explains that need. Scriptures should not only be read to him, but also explained. The following is an example of the way I usually explain the meaning of this scripture:

Romans 5:12 says, *Wherefore, as by one man sin entered into the world, and death by sin; and so death passed upon all men, for that all have sinned.* This "one man" refers to Adam, the man God created. When Adam transgressed against the law of God, sin entered into the world, making all men guilty of what Adam had done. As a result death came upon all mankind.

Sin, by definition, means to miss the mark. When an arrow shot from a bow hits the target but not the center of the bull's eye, we would say the arrow "missed the mark." It is separated by some distance from the bull's eye. That separation represents a gap, or gulf, between the center and the arrow.

When Adam sinned, he caused all men born after him to miss the mark of God. God is located in one place, spiritually speaking; man is in another. The separation between them is spiritual death. This condition points out man's need to know Jesus Christ, the only Person Who can bring man back into union with God to experience the life of God.

As Romans 5:12 says, . . . *and so death passed upon all men, for that all have sinned.* This scripture is not referring to acts of transgression such as murder, lying, cheating, etc., but rather to the condition into which man was born as a result of Adam's sin. Man has sinned simply by virtue of his birth, not because of what he has done.

Before a person receives Jesus Christ as Lord and Savior, he is like a radio which, though in perfect working condition, is unplugged from the source of electricity. Until joined to the source of power, it is essentially dead. This is the hopeless condition of all those who do not know Jesus Christ. It takes Jesus to bridge the gap and connect them with the source of life, God.

To be a Christian does not mean to belong to a certain church or denomination. It means to be in right relationship with God; to be spiritually alive or connected with God, as Christ is.

When ministering salvation to a candidate, you should explain the condition of alienation from God. The concept of salvation is much easier for the person to grasp if you explain that he (or she) is a sinner because of **how** he was born, not **what** he has done. By explaining that he can become a child of God because of what Jesus did, you give him something to look forward to, not dread losing.

If you say he has to give up all the bad things he is doing, he will likely say, "I'll be giving up something and gaining nothing in return." But if you show him what an alienated, separated condition from God really is, he can see that he has nothing to give up. Then you can explain how by receiving Jesus Christ he gains life and all that life has to give. That gives him inspiration and a desire to receive what you have to offer. Few people will reject Jesus Christ when salvation is presented to them this way.

Present the solution to the need.

The lost or unsaved person is separated from the source of life—God— and alienated from his Creator. So, how does he solve this problem? John 3:16 gives the solution: *For God so loved the world, that he gave his only begotten Son, that whosoever believeth in him should not perish, but have everlasting life.* The solution is found in God's Son, Jesus Christ.

Notice two words in this verse: *gave* and *whosoever*. The word *gave* tells us that the solution is a gift, something from God to man without charge. The word *whosoever* tells us the gift is for you. Regardless of your age, sex, race, family background, or social standing, you qualify for the gift God has given—the solution to the world's problems.

Visualize man as a radio with all the necessary equipment to make it operate. Visualize God as the electrical outlet, or source of power. Jesus Christ is the extension cord connecting the radio to the outlet and carrying the power. Jesus is the only connection between God and man. Man cannot know God without knowing Jesus. Jesus said, . . . *no man cometh unto the Father, but by me* (John 14:6). This connection to the source of power is, in essence, the connection of man to the source of true life, which is God.

Explain that salvation is by grace, through faith—a gift.

There are three essential aspects of salvation which the candidate must understand.

1. Receiving Jesus Christ is a work of grace on the part of God.

For by **grace** *are ye saved through faith . . .* (Eph. 2:8). This means God favors man without his deserving that favor. Grace is the equivalent of God's having given us something without our working for it. Those receiving Jesus Christ need to know that they can do nothing to earn Him.

Ephesians 2:9 says our salvation comes, *Not of works, lest any man should boast.* No one is saved because he does "good works." There is no "right" church he can join, no "right" people he can know, no "good" thing he can possibly accomplish that would cause him to merit salvation. The gift of salvation is by grace only. God does not save us because we are good, but because He is good.

2. Receiving the gift of salvation is an act of faith on our part.

One of the simplest methods of acting in faith is to say and do what the Bible says without regard to how we feel. We are saved *through faith*, which means we come into a knowledge of Jesus Christ (or a union with God) by simply finding out what the Bible says; then saying, believing, and doing it, in spite of feelings.

If we believe what we say and do, we are acting in faith—all that is required to receive Jesus Christ.

3. Receiving salvation through Jesus Christ is receiving a gift.

Ephesians 2:8 says salvation is the gift of God. We cannot pay for a gift. We can only return to the giver loving thanks. All we can give God for His gift of Jesus Christ is an expression of thanks and the keeping of His commandments.

According to John 1:12, this gift must be received. *But as many as received him* (Jesus), *to them gave he power to become the sons of God, even to them that believe on his name.* Jesus Christ cannot be forced on anyone; He must be received willingly.

Lead the person to receive the solution, Jesus Christ.

There are two things one must do to receive Jesus Christ. . . . *if thou shalt confess with thy mouth the Lord Jesus, and shalt believe in thine heart that God hath raised him from the dead, thou shalt be saved* (Rom. 10:9).

The word *confess* means to acknowledge, agree with, or say the same thing as another. A person must acknowledge, agree with, and say the same thing that the Bible says about Jesus Christ. What *does* the Bible say about Jesus? That He is Lord and God has raised Him from the dead. To be saved we must acknowledge Jesus Christ as our Lord and believe in our hearts that God has raised Him from the dead. Salvation is a combination of what one says and believes.

No one can make a judgment as to what a person believes in his heart. Only God can do that. In witnessing to someone, we should not concern ourselves with whether he believes what he is saying. We must leave that up to God. If he says he believes Jesus is Lord, it is our responsibility to pray for him, not condemn him.

Many people use 1 John 1:9 in leading a person to Jesus. Technically, this verse was not intended for salvation. It was directed to the Church and was written to urge believers to **repent** of their sins and renew their fellowship with Jesus after they sinned. It says:

If we (believers) *confess our sins, he is faithful and just to forgive us* (believers) *our sins, and to cleanse us* (believers) *from all* (our) *unrighteousness.*

The sinner has never been instructed to confess sin(s); however, he has been directed to acknowledge that he is a sinner. (Rom. 3:23.) Remember, before a person receives Jesus as Lord, the devil is his lord, or spiritual father. (John 8:44; 2 Cor. 4:4.) So, the basic need of a person receiving Jesus as Savior is to denounce the lordship of the devil and receive the lordship of Jesus.

The method of obtaining or receiving the solution of Jesus Christ is to say with your mouth what you believe in your heart: "Jesus is my Lord. I believe God has raised Him from the dead, and He lives in me now."

How to Pray for those Desiring Salvation

First, be sure to pray **with** the candidate, not just for him. Secondly, **lead** him in prayer—instruct him to repeat the prayer you are reciting. Thirdly, base the prayer upon the **Word of God.** It should be a scriptural prayer, such as this:

Dear God,

I come to you, recognizing that I am a sinner in need of acknowledging Jesus Christ as my Lord.

I now turn to Jesus. I believe that He died, was raised from the dead, and now lives. I receive Him as my Lord and Savior.

Jesus, You are my Lord. I am now a new creature in Christ and a child of my heavenly Father, in Jesus' name. Amen.

This prayer should always be consciously based upon God's Word. It begins with "Dear God" because at this point, the person is not a child of God but a creation of God. Technically, he knows God not as heavenly Father, only as Creator.

The first step is getting the person to see himself as a sinner, separated from God, with a need to confess or acknowledge Jesus as his Lord. The statement, "I now turn to Jesus Christ," is another way of saying, "I repent." Then he confesses Romans 10:9. The next phrase, "I receive Him as my Lord and Savior," is based upon John 1:12. The last sentence is an acknowledgment of 2 Corinthians 5:17, *Therefore if any man be in Christ, he is a new creature*, and also that God is now his heavenly Father.

The scriptures given above are simply foundational scriptures. There are many other verses one can use, such as Romans 3:10-13,23; Ephesians 2:1-4; Acts 4:12; 10:43; 16:31; and John 7:30,31.

How to Minister Assurance of Salvation

Ministering assurance of salvation helps those individuals who, at one time, acknowledged Jesus as Lord; but now have doubts within themselves about the experience. Since they may not now **feel** they received Him, they are not sure if they are saved.

Others need assurance because of their misconception of what determines Christianity. They have been taught that to be a Christian means going to church and following the instructions of a denomination. They, however, may have never truly received Jesus as Lord of their lives. After being exposed to the Word of God and the convicting power of the Holy Spirit, they are now aware that something is missing in their lives, because they have never had a real personal relationship with Jesus Christ. Three areas should be emphasized when ministering to such individuals:

1. One must receive Jesus Christ by faith, not by feelings. (2 Cor. 5:7.)

2. Confessing with the mouth and believing with the heart that Jesus is Lord will result in salvation. (Rom. 10:9; 1 John 4:15.) If a person has done this, he must believe that God has been faithful to do what He said He would do: cause him to become a new creation in Christ Jesus.

3. Salvation is current, a present-tense

fact; not something to be received in the future. (1 John 5:11-13; John 3:36.)

How To Pray for those Needing Assurance of Salvation

The following is a scripturally based prayer designed for the person needing assurance of salvation. Have him repeat it after you:

Heavenly Father,

Your Word says that if I confess with my mouth the Lord Jesus and believe in my heart that You raised Him from the dead, I shall be saved. I have done this; so I thank You that I am saved according to Your Word.

You also said that if I confess my sins, You will forgive me. I thank You for forgiving me of any sins I may have committed, in Jesus' name. Amen.

This prayer is to be prayed by the person **after** discovering that he has already received and acknowledged Jesus Christ. If, after ministering scriptures for assurance of salvation, you discover that the person does not have a personal experience with the Lord, then minister salvation as if for the first time.

Note: The prayer of agreement in receiving assurance of salvation is a prayer affirming what the candidate has already received. Included within this prayer is a confession that one's sins will be forgiven based upon 1 John 1:9. If a person is saved, but in doubt about his salvation, chances are the devil has already made him feel condemned. When one feels condemned, he usually resorts to committing some sort of sin.

Additional Scripture references for ministering assurance of salvation: John 3:18; 5:24; 6:47; 1 John 3:1,2.

How to Minister the Gift of the Holy Spirit

There are six foundational Scripture references on how to minister the Holy Spirit. (Other references will be used, but only as support for these.)

1. John 14:16,17,26
2. Luke 11:9-13
3. Acts 1:8
4. Acts 2:4
5. Acts 10:44-46
6. Acts 19:2-6

Inform the candidate of the two qualifications necessary to receive the gift of the Holy Spirit.

In chapter 14 of John, Jesus was speaking to His disciples about the gift of the Holy Spirit. He told them He would pray the Father to send the Comforter to abide with them forever. (v. 16.) We know this "Comforter" is the Holy Spirit, because verse 26 refers to Him as *the Comforter, which is the Holy Ghost.* Jesus was obviously teaching us that once a person receives the gift of the Spirit, He remains with that person forever. He does not come and go.

Verse 17 gives us the first qualification for receiving the Person of the Holy Spirit when it refers to Him as *the Spirit of truth; whom the world cannot receive.* Who is "the world"? The unsaved—those who are out of the Body of Christ. This verse is saying that the unsaved cannot receive the Spirit of Truth (another name for the Holy Spirit).

This is a beautiful scripture to point out to those who claim that the gift of the Holy Spirit is received at salvation. It reveals that the infilling of the Holy Spirit can only be received by those who are **in Christ Jesus.** To receive the Spirit of Truth (the Holy Spirit), the first thing one must do is be born again. The New Birth qualifies a person to receive this precious gift.

The second qualification is found in Luke 11:9-13. *Ask, and it shall be given you . . . every one that asketh receiveth . . . .* We must be receptive. When we **ask the Father** for this gift of the Holy Spirit, He will give Him to us.

This qualification is too simple for some to accept as true. They believe that to receive the gift of the Holy Spirit one must go through a personal purging in his life—taking off certain "clothes" and putting on others; doing various kinds of religious rituals; conforming to this or that standard.

The Bible is plain in its qualifications for receiving the Holy Spirit: (1) Be out of the world and in the Body of Christ. (2) Ask for Him.

If a person has received Christ and is willing to ask for the Holy Spirit, he qualifies. If there is sin in his life, he must, of course, do what 1 John 1:9 instructs—confess it. Jesus will be faithful and just to forgive him. Then he can receive the gift of the Holy Spirit with no hindrance.

Another Scripture reference which supports the second qualification of asking the Father for the gift of the Holy Spirit is 1 John 5:14,15. This is a favorite of mine because it helped set me free. It is one of the best faith scriptures I know.

And this is the confidence that we have in him, that, if we ask any thing according to his will, he heareth us: And if we know that he hear us, whatsoever we ask, we know that we have the petitions that we desired of him.

If we ask anything according to God's will, we don't have to wonder whether He will hear us. This says very plainly, . . . *he heareth us.* A person should be told that when he asks for the gift of the Holy Spirit, God hears him the first time he asks because his request is made according to God's will, which is the Word. It is God's will for all His children to receive the gift of the Holy Spirit. When we know that He hears us, we know we **have**—present tense—our petition. Although the person may not see any tangible evidence of the gift, it is a faith fact; he has the petition he desired.

This scripture is exciting to me because it lets us know that we can claim what we have requested according to God's will. This is how a person should be instructed. When he has asked for that which is in God's Word, he can claim, by faith, that he has the petition—confidently declaring that he has received the gift of the Holy Spirit. Though he has not yet spoken with other tongues, he should verbally say, "By faith, I **believe** I have received the gift of the Holy Spirit. The physical evidence will manifest."

Show the candidate the reason for receiving this gift.

There is one primary reason for receiving the Holy Spirit: to have, or be endued with, supernatural power. When a person receives Jesus Christ, he receives the measure of the Holy Spirit in salvation. To that degree he has supernatural power, but there is more power yet to be received. The salvation experience results in obtaining eternal life and an earthly relationship with the living God, but one needs to experience the fullness of the power of the Holy Spirit in order to exercise authority over the supernatural ability of the enemy.

Acts 1:8 says, *But ye shall receive power, after that the Holy Ghost is come upon you.* If a person does not have the Holy Spirit, he does not have this power. Receiving the gift of the Holy Spirit enables the believer to be a more effective witness in this earth realm.

There are other benefits, but the primary one is this supernatural power. The Greek word for "power" is *dunamis,* meaning God endues us with dynamite, megaton-bomb power to do the work with Him. It takes this kind of supernatural ability to work with the Lord as we should.

Explain to the candidate what he should expect to do after receiving this precious gift.

When the disciples received the gift of the Holy Spirit at Pentecost, *they began to speak with other tongues, as the Spirit gave them utterance* (Acts 2:4). Acts 10:46 says that when Peter and his companions witnessed of Christ to Cornelius and his group, *they heard them speak with tongues, and magnify God* when the Spirit fell upon them. Acts 19:6 says that when Paul laid his hands on the believers in Ephesus, *the Holy Ghost came on them; and they spake with tongues, and prophesied.*

It is a good idea to have the candidate read these verses with you. Direct him to emphasize the passage of Scripture that refers to speaking with other tongues. The Bible says, *So then faith cometh by hearing, and hearing by the word of God* (Rom. 10:17).

As he hears himself read these scriptures that say he should speak with other tongues, his faith will be elevated to expect it to happen.

Lead the candidate to receive the Spirit by faith.

At this point, most people are ready to follow in a prayer of agreement to receive the gift of the Holy Spirit. If not, perhaps a review of the scriptures would help. Also, it may be good to use other references— 1 Corinthians 14:2-4,18; Isaiah 28:11,12; Mark 16:17.

If the candidate is ready to pray, instruct him as follows:

First, remind him of 1 John 5:14,15— that if he asks anything according to God's will, He will hear him—so he can consider himself as having already received that which he has asked. Rehearse with him 1 John 5:15 that says when something is asked of God according to His will, He hears the first time; the request need not be repeated.

Secondly, remind him that, as far as God is concerned, he already has the petition he desired. It is important to explain to him that by faith he must believe after he has prayed.

How To Pray for those Desiring the Gift of the Holy Spirit

Have him repeat this prayer:

Heavenly Father,

You said if I would ask for the Holy Spirit, You would give Him to me. I'm asking You now to fill me with the Holy Spirit.

Holy Spirit, I receive You.

Thank You, Father, that I am now going to speak with other tongues as the Spirit gives me utterance. According to Your Word I believe I have received the infilling of the Holy Spirit, in Jesus' name. Amen.

Lead the candidate to release the utterance God gives him.

After he has repeated the prayer to receive the Holy Spirit, ask him, "Do you believe you have received the gift of the Holy Spirit, although you may not have physically spoken with other tongues?" After he has confirmed his belief that he has received the Spirit, instruct him to open his mouth and begin to speak, expecting the Holy Spirit to cooperate with his act of faith and give a supernatural articulation or utterance.

Usually the greatest challenge for believers who are ministering the Holy

Spirit is to get the candidate to express in other tongues that which he has received by faith. It is important that very clear instructions be given. Confusion or lack of understanding can hinder the person from receiving the flow of utterance.

Note Acts 2:4 again. *And they . . . began to speak with other tongues, as the Spirit gave them utterance.* Who began to speak? **They**—the people. The Holy Ghost didn't speak; the people spoke. He gave the articulation, or made clear what was spoken, but the people did the speaking.

This is an important point which many have not fully understood, causing them problems in receiving the evidence of speaking in other tongues.

The candidate must be told that it is his responsibility to open his mouth and begin to speak. He should know, when he does this, that it is not anything supernatural **initially.** The natural man is speaking. The supernatural is related not to his speaking, but to what he ultimately says when he speaks. God will take what he begins to speak forth and formulate words not learned in school nor understood. These words are what the Bible calls ''other tongues.''

As he opens his mouth and begins to speak, he must know it is an act of faith. He is doing what the Bible says to do—beginning to speak—with the expectation that the Holy Spirit will give him supernatural utterances he would not otherwise have. He should be told not to speak words he already knows. If he is English-speaking, he should not speak English. If he is Spanish-speaking, he should not speak Spanish.

This is an act of his faith, but also of his flesh. He is speaking words in the natural. But this physical effort results in the Holy Spirit taking his tongue and forming a supernatural language, one he does not know and has never known. These utterances may not sound like a language, but there are thousands of dialects no one person would ever begin to know.

The one ministering the Holy Spirit should also pray with other tongues, encouraging the person to continue acting in faith by speaking with the expectation of the supernatural utterance to come forth.

Sometimes, a candidate may feel inhibited about releasing these sounds. He may think it doesn't make sense to do something that appears foolish before others; or he may be shy. When ministering to such a person, do all you can to encourage him to act in faith, disregarding what others may think. This encouragement should be made with tenderness, consideration, patience, and love. Many will immediately receive a supernatural utterance. Others will receive a few seconds or minutes after praying. Some may take longer.

Although a person may not receive a physical utterance in tongues after a week, a month, or even two months, he should be instructed to confess with his mouth what he believes in his heart—that, based upon God's Word, he has, by faith, the petition he desired of God.

The important thing is for the person to be encouraged. Instruct him to continue standing in faith, confessing with his mouth and believing in his heart that he has received the gift of the Holy Spirit and is now waiting for the physical manifestation of speaking with other tongues to come forth.

When instructions are given clearly, most candidates who truly want to receive the gift of the Holy Spirit will receive, with the full manifestation of His presence as evidenced by speaking in other tongues.

I worked with one candidate for three weeks before she received this evidence. We met together about a half-hour each week for counseling and prayer. During this period she confessed continually, "I believe according to the Word of God that I have already received the gift of the Holy Spirit, and I expect to speak with other tongues at any time." So she did.

This is not what some refer to as "tarrying." There is no need to tarry or wait for the Holy Spirit. The Bible says the Holy Spirit abides with us now. All we need do is open our hearts and mouths to receive what God has already provided through Jesus Christ.

While praying for a person to receive the gift of the Holy Spirit, your hand should be laid upon his forehead, if possible. Different techniques are used to encourage him to relax his tongue so the Holy Spirit can take control of it. Believe God for the wisdom necessary to help one release the utterance.

Instruct the candidate to pray in tongues daily.

On the day of Pentecost, the Christians did not have the New Testament as we do today to receive specific knowledge concerning various areas of spiritual truths. They simply believed and received what God had provided for them. Today we can also believe and receive. Many have simply received the Holy Spirit, with no instructions whatsoever. To others, it has not been so simple. This is why God has revealed technical truths from His Word to help those desiring to receive the best from Him.

Just as there are many ways God manifests divine healing to His children, so there are many ways He manifests the gift of the Holy Spirit. The important point is not how it is accomplished, but the fact that it happens. The main objective is to receive power with the evidence of speaking in tongues, to have the privilege of praying to the heavenly Father in a language He has given to edify and build up the spirit man, and to receive the revelation He desires us to have.

After the person has spoken with other tongues, he should be instructed to pray in tongues at will, just as he prays in his native language at will. First Corinthians 14:15 says: *What is it then? I will pray with the spirit, and I will pray with the understanding also.* The word *will* shows that it is our choice. We can pray with the Spirit (in other tongues) as we choose; we can pray with the understanding as we choose. Once the Holy Spirit is in us, it is simply a matter of opening our mouths and letting Him flow out.

The Holy Spirit is a living infinite Person; never stagnant, but always ready and willing to manifest His power through us. John 7:38,39 describes the Holy Spirit as a river of living water. A lake is stationary, but a river moves at all times. The only way to stop the flow of a river is to dam it up. The only way the flow of the Holy Spirit in us can be dammed up is for us to shut our mouths and not let Him come out. The moment we open our mouths the river or power starts flowing again. It's just a question of whether or not we let Him express Himself in an outward utterance.

This is why the candidate should be encouraged to pray in other tongues two or three times initially after receiving the gift of the Holy Spirit. He then can realize that he has control over releasing the power God just gave him, and will develop confidence that the utterance will come forth when he is on his own. All he need do is release that power by opening his mouth and speaking. As an act of faith he should expect the Holy Spirit to give utterances that would not normally come forth.

There will be a noticeable difference in the sounds or utterance the Holy Spirit gives. This difference in utterance can be termed a divine experience. The candidate will have an inner witness that something divine has happened. Until he experiences this divine release of utterance, he should confess that he believes he has already received the Holy Spirit by faith and is now waiting for the physical evidence of a divine utterance in other tongues.

Additional Scripture references for ministering the gift of the Holy Spirit: 1 Corinthians 14:2-4,18; Isaiah 28:11,12; Mark 16:17.

Frank L. Stewart, a graduate of Pepperdine University at Los Angeles, California, has over twenty years of experience as a minister of the gospel. The development of Frank's practical knowledge of leadership skills has come through several positions held in the private sector as well as in churches.

Frank is the founder and president of Frank Stewart Ministries, Inc., ZOE Christian Leadership Training Center and ZOE Christian Fellowship (Church). ZOE Christian Training Center is a unique Bible-based system providing personal leadership training through an intensive and concise curriculum that emphasizes personal management skills and instruction in how each Christian can discover his place in the Body of Christ.

These multi-faceted ministries are being used as vehicles to touch the lives of many people on a local, national and international basis. Located in Los Angeles, California, Frank Stewart and ZOE Ministries continue to grow rapidly as a service to the Body of Christ.

Write: Frank Stewart • P. O. Box 5959D • Los Angeles, CA 90059

How To Share The New Birth
and The Gift of the Holy Spirit
is available at your local bookstore.

Harrison House • P. O. Box 35035 • Tulsa, OK 74153